Rich Off Credit:
Why Access Matters More Than Money

by

Jahvain Royalty

Fort Lauderdale, Florida

Rich Off Credit
Copyright © 2026 Jahvain Royalty

For more info, contact the author at:

ISBN: 978-1-7355723-2-1 (paperback)
ISBN: 978-1-7355723-3-8 (ebook)

Library of Congress Control Number: 2026936965

Printed in the United States of America

DEDICATION

To my family who has always supported me

C O N T E N T S

There are books you read once, and there are books that quietly alter how you see the world. Not because of hype or trends, and not because of clever marketing, but because certain knowledge only arrives when the reader is ready to receive it.

Whether you purchased it, borrowed it, stumbled across a screenshot, or had someone insist you read it, if this book found its way to you, understand this clearly: **its arrival was not accidental**. Timing, not coincidence, is what brings a book like this into your hands. A particular version of you is awake now. One that refuses to live small, that is exhausted by survival alone, and that senses life is meant to operate on a larger scale than bills, routines, and quiet resignation.

You were never lacking ambition.
You were lacking the blueprint.

This is not a book about getting rich quickly, nor is it a collection of motivational slogans dressed up as strategy. It is not written for spectators, dabblers, or those looking for surface-level inspiration. It is written for people who have worked hard, played by the rules they were given, and still found themselves blocked – confused by why effort did not translate into access.

The answer is simpler than most people realize.

This book is not truly about money. Money is only the visible layer. What governs outcomes is access: who is trusted, who is predictable, and who is permitted to move with leverage inside systems most people never learn to read. Credit is merely the doorway. Beyond it sits power: the kind that shapes opportunity before opportunity ever appears.

These systems are not taught in school. They are rarely explained clearly. And they are almost never discussed honestly within families. Instead, they are learned quietly, often privately, and passed down as operational knowledge from one generation of wealth to the next.

The chapters ahead are designed to make that hidden architecture legible.

You will learn how the system actually evaluates you, how identity is recorded and interpreted, and why two people with the same income can experience entirely different outcomes. You will learn why discipline matters more than income, why structure matters more than motivation, and why most people remain stuck not because they are incapable, but because they are misaligned.

This book does not ask you to become someone else. It teaches you how to become visible to the systems that already govern access. Once that happens, progress stops feeling random. Denials stop feeling personal. And movement becomes intentional rather than hopeful.

Take a breath.

Turn the page.

What follows is not theory for entertainment. It is a map—one designed to help you move with clarity, precision, and control inside a system that has always been watching, measuring, and responding.

Welcome to the beginning of your real education.

INTRODUCTION

Why Access Matters More Than Money

This book is structured differently than most financial books because it is solving a different problem.

Most financial advice assumes that information is the barrier. That if people simply knew more about budgeting, saving, or investing, for instance, they would make better decisions and achieve better outcomes. In reality, most people already know what they are *supposed* to do. What they do not understand is why effort, income, and intelligence often fail to translate into access.

This book addresses that gap.

At its core, *Rich Off Credit* is an exploration of how modern financial systems evaluate trust, predict behavior, and decide who is allowed to move with leverage. Credit is not treated here as a consumer product or a score to be chased. It is examined as infrastructure: a system of rules, data, and identity that quietly governs opportunity long before money ever enters the picture.

To make that system usable, the book unfolds in deliberate stages.

Part I establishes the foundation. It explains how credit actually works beneath the surface: how identity is recorded, how behavior is translated into data, and how decisions are made algorithmically rather than personally. You will learn why credit functions less like judgment and more like law, why most people misunderstand what their score represents, and how hidden data systems influence outcomes even when traditional reports appear clean.

Part II shifts from understanding to correction. Here, the focus is on restoring alignment. Credit damage is treated not as a moral failure or a waiting game, but as a data problem with procedural solutions. This section outlines how informed borrowers repair profiles in ways institutions respect, why certain disputes succeed while others fail, and how restoration becomes momentum when handled strategically.

Part III explains how access turns into capital. This is where credit stops being defensive and becomes productive. You will learn how funding actually scales, why banks treat long-term relationships differently than isolated applications, and how personal and business credit function together rather than in competition. The emphasis here is progression—moving through stages intentionally instead of stalling at surface-level milestones.

Part IV addresses posture and discipline. Access without control creates volatility. This section examines the internal rules that determine whether leverage compounds or collapses. It is not about motivation, but about operating principles—how people who retain access think, move, and respond to pressure once the system begins to work in their favor.

Part V extends the lens beyond the individual. Wealth that ends with one person is not wealth; it is consumption delayed. The final section explores how access, identity, and structure compound across time, families, and generations, and why systems, not individuals, are what ultimately endure.

This book is designed to be read in order. Each section builds on the last, and skipping ahead often removes the context that makes later strategies effective. The goal is not to overwhelm, but to replace confusion with clarity so that approvals stop feeling random, denials stop feeling personal, and progress becomes something you can engineer rather than hope for.

The pages that follow will not ask you to work harder or believe blindly. They will ask you to see clearly.

The Prologue that follows does not begin with theory, but with proof.

PROLOGUE

The Secret They Kept Out of School

Your life is about to change, not because you decided to work harder or hustle longer, but because you are about to understand something school was never designed to teach you. Once you grasp why credit was excluded from the classroom, the system begins to make sense. Access was always the real mechanism. Money was always the illusion.

Most books begin by telling you what to do. This one begins with a story, because understanding credit requires context before instruction. It requires seeing how the system works on real lives, not just spreadsheets.

Marcus Redd was 32 years old, a father of two, working overnight security at a distribution warehouse in Georgia. He never made more than $15 an hour. His hands were rough, his eyes perpetually tired, and his back ached in ways that sleep never fully repaired. Each morning, he walked three miles home because he didn't own a car. By every traditional measure, Marcus was broke. No one would have looked at him and imagined a future landlord, investor, or business owner.

His life didn't change because of a mentor, an inheritance, or a lucky break. It changed because of an algorithm.

After being declined for yet another apartment, Marcus sat on a cracked bus stop bench and asked a question most people never stop to ask: *If I'm working, why does the system still treat me like I don't exist?* That night, on an aging laptop, he discovered something that altered his trajectory. Credit did not begin as money. Credit began as trust that was recorded.

Long before cash existed, people borrowed time. Farmers borrowed seed before harvest. Merchants borrowed goods before trade routes closed. Kings borrowed armies before wars were won. Repayment was delayed, not immediate. That agreement to pay later was the earliest form of credit. At first, trust lived in faces and handshakes. Then it moved to written promises, then to ledgers, then to courts. As societies grew, trust shifted from people to paper, from relationships to rules.

Banks didn't invent money. They perfected credit. They realized they didn't need to own all the wealth; they only needed to control access to it. Over time, credit became standardized, digitized, and automated. Today, no single person decides your financial future. Data does.

Payment history, utilization, account age, inquiries, public records, and identity markers all combine into a profile that predicts behavior. Credit is not a moral judgment. It is a mathematical one. It measures predictability, not worth.

That realization changed Marcus's life. He understood that his credit score was not a grade. It was a key, and keys open doors.

He learned how access unfolds in stages. A score around 680 opens doors. Around 720 creates leverage. Around 760 unlocks capital. At 800, systems begin to work in your favor. Marcus didn't become a genius overnight, nor did his income suddenly explode. He aligned his behavior with the rules of the credit system.

A $300 secured card became a $1,000 limit. That $1,000 became $5,000. That $5,000 became a $24,000 American Express line. Limits became business funding. Business funding became car rentals. Cashflow followed. Cashflow became a real estate down payment. Equity created more equity. One door led to another.

Marcus didn't start rich. He didn't start connected. He didn't start special. He started with a file, a file the system used to judge him until he learned how to rewrite it.

This book exists so you can do the same, faster and with fewer mistakes. You will not learn credit the way consumers do. You will learn it the way creators of credit do, by understanding the architecture behind the decisions.

Once you see the system clearly, you stop asking for permission. You start moving with precision.

PART I

THE SCIENCE, SPIRIT, AND SECRET ARCHITECTURE OF CREDIT

1

CREDIT IS THE MODERN-DAY DIVINE LAW

Most people believe money runs the world. It doesn't. Credit does. Money is physical and visible, something you can hold in your hand or watch leave your account. Credit is less obvious but far more powerful. It determines what you are allowed to command, not just what you can purchase today, but what becomes possible tomorrow.

Money reacts to the present. Credit shapes the future. One buys what is available now; the other quietly defines the scope of your options. You may not see credit when you walk into a bank, tap a card, or receive an approval notification, but it is always there, operating beneath the surface. Invisible, measurable, predictive, psychological, behavioral, and algorithmic, credit is the silent force evaluating you long before you ever make a request.

Before understanding the technical mechanics of credit, you must understand the law beneath it. Because whether you frame it as divine order, universal principle, or mathematical logic, one truth holds: credit rewards alignment and punishes chaos. It functions like any other governing system. Patterns are observed, recorded, and responded to consistently.

The credit system does not care about your explanations. It does not respond to emotion, intent, or effort. It responds to behavior repeated over time. What matters is not what happened once, but what happens predictably. That is why credit decisions feel impersonal. They are.

It cares about your patterns:

- Pay consistently → doors open
- Pay late and emotional → doors close
- Use credit for liabilities → stay trapped
- Use credit for assets → escape

Those four lines explain more about credit outcomes than most financial courses ever will.

In older civilizations, divine laws were carved into stone so people could see them and live accordingly. In the modern world, those laws are written into data. Every swipe, every payment, every missed due date, every balance carried forward contributes to a pattern the system learns to trust or avoid. Credit is not a score in isolation. It is a living record of how you move through obligation.

To understand this more clearly, consider a parable.

The Two Sons

A wealthy merchant had two sons. As he grew older, he decided to test their understanding of value. To the first son, he gave a heavy bag of gold. To the second, he extended a line of credit in his name.

The first son felt rich immediately. He had never held that much money before. He bought clothes, hosted feasts, and surrounded himself with people who praised and admired him. The second son felt pressure instead of excitement. He didn't possess the money outright; he only had access to it. So he used that access to buy inventory, build supplier relationships, and open trade accounts. He sold goods, reinvested the profits, and repeated the process.

The gold eventually ran out. The access multiplied.

Three years later, the first son was broke, bitter, and blaming circumstance. The second controlled warehouses, trade routes, and supply chains that sustained entire neighborhoods. When the merchant called them to his bedside, he explained the difference simply. Gold makes a person comfortable for a moment. Credit makes a person unstoppable over time.

That distinction sits at the heart of this book.

Credit is more than a score. It is a contract between your past behavior and your future access. Every action feeds that agreement. The system does not ask why you struggled. It observes whether you adapted. It does not care about motivation. It measures consistency.

This is where the divide appears. Powerful people use credit as leverage, a tool designed to multiply effort and accelerate outcomes. Average people use credit as a lifestyle crutch, something to soften discomfort without changing structure. The same system responds very differently to those two approaches.

When you understand this, credit stops feeling personal. It becomes legible. And once it becomes legible, it becomes usable.

You are not about to learn credit as a consumer, hoping for approval. You are about to learn it as someone who understands the law behind the approval. When you can read the data the way the system reads you, you stop guessing and start moving with precision.

2

THE 5 FINANCIAL IDENTITIES — WHY MOST PEOPLE STAY POOR

Everyone has a financial identity, whether they are aware of it or not. It is not the story you tell yourself about who you are with money, nor the intentions you hold when you make decisions. It is the story the system tells about you based entirely on what it can observe, verify, and predict.

Your financial identity determines how you are treated by lenders, landlords, employers, and institutions. It decides who gets access, who gets leverage, and who remains invisible. Most people never realize this identity exists, which is why they feel confused when their effort and income don't translate into opportunity. The system is not responding to potential. It is responding to identity.

Your financial identity is made of five layers:

1. **Personal Credit Identity**
   This is your FICO soul, the grade assigned to you in the eyes of consumer lenders. It reflects payment history, utilization, account age, and inquiries, and it serves as the first filter through which most approvals are decided.

2. **Business Credit Identity**
   This is your corporate double, an entity with scaling potential far beyond your personal profile when structured correctly. It allows you to borrow, grow, and leverage without placing constant pressure on your personal credit file.

3. **Banking Relationship Identity**
   This is your reputation inside each bank's private risk system. It

is not your FICO score. It is an internal score based on your deposit behavior, account management, overdraft history, and overall relationship with the institution. You rarely see it, but banks rely on it heavily.

4. **Income & Documentation Identity**
   This layer reflects what you can prove on paper. Tax returns, pay stubs, bank statements, and documented business revenue determine how real and reliable you appear to the system, regardless of how much money you actually make.

5. **Behavioral Identity**
   This is how predictable, disciplined, and safe you appear over time. It is shaped by patterns, not moments, and it quietly influences every decision made about your access to credit and capital.

The average person only understands the first layer. They reduce their entire financial existence to a single question: do I have good credit or bad credit? That narrow view keeps them trapped, because improving one layer while ignoring the others rarely produces meaningful change. Wealthy individuals understand all five and align them intentionally.

To see how this plays out in real life, consider the story of Elisa.

Elisa was a hairstylist in Houston earning between $6,000 and $8,000 a month, almost entirely in cash. To her clients, she looked successful. To her family, she was doing well. To herself, she felt close but not secure. To the financial system, she barely existed.

On paper, it appeared she earned nothing. There were no W-2s, no tax returns showing real income, and no consistent deposits in her personal account. Apartments saw her as risky. Auto lenders saw her as unstable. Despite perfect payment history on her personal cards, low utilization, and a stable address, her identity layers were misaligned.

Once she documented her income properly and began moving like a financial adult, everything shifted. Her score rose from the low 600s into the 700s. She received her first American Express card, then her first business card. She formed an LLC, opened a business checking account, and began depositing income consistently. With proper tax filing and strategic write-offs, she secured a $15,000 business line and grew her monthly revenue to $18,000 within five months.

Nothing about Elisa changed except how the system saw her.

That is the central lesson of this chapter. Your financial identity is not who you are. It is who the system believes you are. And the system pays based on its perception, not your effort, your talent, or your potential.

The good news is that identity is editable. When you understand the layers and align them deliberately, the system responds. This book is not asking you to become someone else. It is teaching you how to become legible to the system that already governs access.

3

THE INVISIBLE CREDIT BUREAUS YOU'VE NEVER HEARD OF

Most people believe the credit system begins and ends with three names. They check their scores, track minor changes, and assume that if those numbers look good, they are safe. This belief is one of the most expensive misunderstandings in personal finance.

The "Big Three" consumer credit bureaus are:

- Experian
- Equifax
- TransUnion

These bureaus matter, but they are not the whole system. They are the public-facing layer, the part consumers are allowed to see. Behind them exists a quieter, more influential network that most people never learn about until it blocks them.

Behind the Big Three is a web of lesser-known data agencies often referred to as shadow bureaus. These organizations do not focus on scores. They focus on identity, behavior, and risk signals that banks use to make decisions long before your FICO score is considered.

Some of the most influential shadow bureaus include:

- LexisNexis
- SageStream
- ChexSystems
- Early Warning Services
- Innovis
- ARS and similar specialty databases

The credit reporting system, a network of bureaus, data furnishers, and scoring models, does not evaluate intent. It evaluates patterns. Thus, these agencies track information most consumers never think to review. They record address and phone history, identity consistency, banking behavior, past account closures, overdrafts, fraud flags, and public records. They often retain data long after you believe an issue has been resolved.

This hidden layer feeds information into the larger credit ecosystem. Banks use it to approve or deny checking accounts, flag applications as risky, close existing accounts, or reinsert negative information that appears to have been removed. A clean report with the Big Three does not guarantee approval if your shadow profile raises concerns.

To understand how this plays out, consider Carl's experience.

Carl worked hard to repair his credit. He raised his score from the high 500s into the 700s, paid off collections, lowered his utilization, and cleaned up late payments. On paper, his reports looked strong. But every time he tried to open a new checking account or apply for a quality credit card, he was denied.

Frustrated, Carl couldn't understand how a 700-plus score still translated into rejection. What he didn't realize was that years earlier, he had bounced checks, overdrafted accounts repeatedly, and walked away from a closed bank account. That history lived on in ChexSystems and Early Warning Services. While his credit reports looked healthy, his banking identity still read as high risk.

Once Carl addressed those hidden records by settling old balances, requesting updates, submitting goodwill letters, and opening a fresh account with a smaller credit union, the pattern changed. His credit score stayed the same, but his access improved dramatically. The issue had never been his score. It was the data behind it.

This is the lesson most people never learn. You cannot fix what you do not know exists. The system does not judge you based on a single number. It evaluates you through layered data sources that talk to one another quietly and continuously.

Until you understand the shadow bureaus, you are only managing the surface of your financial identity. Mastery comes from cleaning both what you can see and what you cannot. Once you do, denials stop feeling random, and approvals stop feeling like luck.

4

METRO 2: THE SECRET CODING LANGUAGE OF CREDIT

Most people who talk about credit never mention Metro 2. That omission is revealing. It is often the clearest signal that someone understands credit at the surface level but not at the system level. Metro 2 is not a tactic, a dispute trick, or a collection of letter templates. It is the language credit furnishers use to communicate with the bureaus.

When banks report information, they do not write narratives about your behavior. They transmit data encoded into standardized fields, status codes, date markers, and compliance indicators. Those codes determine how your account is interpreted by the credit system long after a human being has stopped paying attention.

Metro 2 is a data standard. It governs how information must be reported, updated, corrected, and resolved. Understanding it is the difference between arguing emotionally with the system and enforcing accuracy within it. The Metro 2 format is the industry-standard data specification established by the Consumer Data Industry Association (CDIA) for reporting consumer credit history to major credit bureaus.

When an account is encoded incorrectly, the consequences are real and often invisible to consumers. Errors in Metro 2 coding can cause a paid account to appear unpaid, a closed account to damage your age of credit, or a resolved collection to look active. Dates can be misreported, balances duplicated, and utilization inflated simply because data was transmitted incorrectly.

These coding errors affect outcomes such as:
- whether an account appears open or closed
- whether it looks current, late, or delinquent
- whether a collection is active, settled, or obsolete
- whether a charge-off appears recent or aged
- whether duplicate accounts appear across reports
- whether utilization appears higher than it actually is

Most consumers respond to these issues by disputing emotionally, explaining hardship, or pleading for goodwill. The system does not respond to any of that. It responds to compliance.

Metro 2 is where credit stops being personal and becomes procedural. You are no longer asking for mercy. You are asserting that reported data must meet federal accuracy standards. This shift changes everything. When you understand how information is supposed to be coded, you stop requesting favors and start enforcing rules.

You do not need to become a programmer or data analyst to use Metro 2 logic effectively. You need to understand what "accurate reporting" actually means under federal guidelines, how compliance timelines work, and how to challenge information based on coding errors rather than narrative explanations. Precision replaces persuasion.

This is why Metro 2 knowledge separates people who see occasional removals from those who see entire profiles transform. When disputes are framed around accuracy and compliance, banks are required to respond differently. They must either correct the data or substantiate it properly. Silence, delay, or vague confirmation is no longer sufficient.

By the time you finish this chapter, you should understand one essential truth: your credit report is not a story about your past. It is a database governed by rules. When you learn those rules, you stop reacting to the system and start navigating it.

This completes the work of Part I. You now understand credit as power, identity, data, and architecture. You know how the system sees you, how information is tracked beyond the surface, and how that information is encoded. With that foundation in place, the next stage is not learning more theory. It is correction.

In **Part II: The Resurrection**, the focus shifts from understanding the system to repairing your position within it. Knowledge becomes action. Alignment becomes restoration.

PART II

THE RESURRECTION: HOW TO REBUILD ANY CREDIT PROFILE IN 90 DAYS

5

RESURRECTION BLUEPRINT — REPAIR YOUR PROFILE THE WAY BANKS SECRETLY PREFER

Most people treat damaged credit like a prison sentence. They assume that once something goes wrong, time is the only cure. Seven years feels like a verdict rather than a reporting window. That belief keeps people passive, waiting for relief instead of reclaiming control.

A damaged credit profile is not a life sentence. It is a data problem. And data problems have structured solutions.

Your credit report is not your identity. It is an editable document. It reflects past behavior, not permanent worth. When people fail to repair their credit, it is rarely because repair is impossible. It is because they approach the system emotionally rather than procedurally.

Before outlining the steps, it helps to see what proper execution looks like in real life.

The Man With 18 Negative Accounts

Deon was 36 years old, a father of two, who lost his job during the pandemic. Bills piled up faster than he could manage them. Eventually, he stopped opening mail, stopped checking balances, and stopped answering unfamiliar phone numbers. By the time he needed a car to pursue a new opportunity, his credit file looked devastating.

He had 18 negative accounts, including multiple charge-offs, collections, a repossession, and late payments spread across two years. His score sat in the high 400s. Most people would have accepted defeat. Deon gave himself 30 minutes to panic, then decided something else instead. If the system could bury him with paperwork, he would learn that paperwork better than the system itself.

What follows is now known as the Resurrection Blueprint.

The Resurrection Blueprint

(The Exact Steps)

Fixing credit is not about attacking everything at once. It is more like surgery. You identify the infection, isolate it, and treat it precisely. The following steps reflect how informed borrowers repair profiles in ways banks respect.

STEP 1: Pull All Three Credit Reports

(The Real Ones)

Not summaries. Not free apps. Not simplified dashboards. You need complete reports from:

- Experian
- Equifax
- TransUnion

Think of this as diagnostic imaging. Until you see the full data, you are guessing.

STEP 2: Clean Your Financial Identity

(Address and Name Reset)

This is the step most people skip, and it is often the most powerful. Reports frequently contain outdated addresses, duplicate entries, misspelled names, old employers, and incorrect phone numbers. Negative accounts are often tied to these identity markers.

When you remove outdated or incorrect identifiers, you can sever the verification link that allows certain negative items to persist. In many cases, collections and duplicate accounts fall away simply because they can no longer be properly matched to your active identity.

This is not cosmetic. It is foundational.

STEP 3: Validate Every Negative Item

(For Accuracy, Not Emotion)

Every negative account must meet legal and reporting standards. Each one should be evaluated against four questions:

1. Is the debt reported accurately under federal law and Metro 2 standards?

2. Is the furnisher compliant with reporting timelines and update requirements?

3. Does the reporting entity have legal standing to report this debt?

4. Can full documentation and chain of ownership be produced?

If the answer to any of these is no, the account must be corrected, re-coded, updated, or removed. This is not about explaining hardship. It is about enforcing accuracy.

STEP 4: Separate Items Into Four Buckets

Professionals do not treat all negative items the same. Each account belongs in one of four categories:

- **Bucket A — Identity Errors**
Wrong person, wrong address, wrong account.

- **Bucket B — Reporting Errors**
Incorrect dates, balances, statuses, or payment history.

- **Bucket C — True but Negotiable Debts**
Legitimate accounts that can be settled, deleted, or favorably updated.

> **• Bucket D — Legitimate Debts You Must Handle**
> Accurate accounts that must be paid or strategically managed.

This step prevents wasted effort and focuses energy where results are possible.

STEP 5: Freeze the Shadow Bureaus

(Prevent Reinsertion Before Cleanup Begins)

Shadow agencies such as LexisNexis, SageStream, Innovis, ARS, and ChexSystems collect, distribute, and cross-match identity and account information behind the scenes. Freezing them limits the ability of outdated or previously deleted data to re-enter your file.

STEP 6: Time Disputes Strategically

(Precision Over Volume)

Credit reporting follows cycles. Timing disputes around furnisher reporting schedules and bureau processing windows increases the chances of successful updates and deletions. Precision matters more than repetition.

STEP 7: Drop Utilization

(The Score Accelerator Once the Dust Settles)

After major negative items are removed, corrected, or updated, it becomes essential to optimize your balance-to-limit ratios. Utilization represents a significant portion of most scoring models:

- under 29%
- under 9%
- 3–7%

STEP 8: Add New Positive Tradelines

(The Credit "Medicine" After the Infection Is Gone)

A rebuilt profile typically includes:

- o   two to three revolving accounts
- o   one installment account
- o   one authorized user account from a perfect profile

STEP 9: Reassess After 90 Days

After a structured repair cycle, your profile should reflect corrected data, lower utilization, active positive tradelines, and aligned identity markers. At this point, your score becomes a tool rather than a limitation.

Deon followed these steps. Ninety days later, his score crossed into the 700s. His access changed. His trajectory changed. The system responded not because it became kinder, but because it was engaged correctly.

In the chapters ahead, we will deepen each of these steps and show how restoration becomes momentum.

PART III

THE FUNDING LADDER — TURNING CREDIT INTO CAPITAL

6

THE 4 STAGES OF FUNDING — HOW THE WEALTHY CLIMB THE LADDER

Every financially powerful person moves through the same four stages of funding. These stages are not tied to personality, income, or intelligence. They are structural. The difference between people who struggle with access and those who move fluidly through opportunity is not effort, but progression.

The four stages are:

Stage 1: Consumer Approval
(Your personal credit foundation)

Stage 2: Relationship-Based Funding
(Banks begin to actually trust you)

Stage 3: Business Credit Leverage
(Your LLC becomes your second social security number)

Stage 4: Capital Scaling
(Large credit lines ☐ assets ☐ cashflow ☐ buy-back of time)

Most people never move beyond Stage 1. They spend their entire financial lives celebrating surface-level milestones, a 700 score, a single major card, or a $10,000 limit, without realizing they have mistaken the starting line for the destination.

Wealthy families think differently. They use personal credit as a launchpad, not a finish line. Your personal profile tells the bank who you are. Your business profile tells the bank what you can build. To understand how the ladder works, each stage must be examined precisely.

Stage 1: Consumer Approval

(The Foundation)

Stage 1 is where lenders decide whether you are safe. Not impressive. Not wealthy. Not powerful. Simply predictable. At this level, the system is not evaluating ambition or potential. It is assessing risk.

The questions being asked are basic but unforgiving:

- Do you pay on time?
- Do you spend responsibly?
- Do you use credit as a tool or as entertainment?
- Do you treat debt like oxygen or like fire?

To advance, your personal credit profile must meet several non-negotiable standards:

✓ **Payment History:** 100% spotless
Even a single late payment damages trust.

✓ **Utilization:** 1–7% (elite zone)
Low enough to show discipline, active enough to show usage.

✓ **Age of Credit:** 3–5 years average
Authorized user tradelines can support this if you are newer.

✓ **Inquiries:** Fewer than 3–4 per bureau
Excessive inquiries signal desperation.

✓ **No Recent Derogatories**
Charge-offs, collections, or repossessions trigger immediate concern.

Stage 1 is not glamorous, but it is foundational. Without it, nothing else works. To see how income alone fails to substitute for discipline, consider Jason's story.

Story: The Man with High Income but No Approvals

Jason earned $180,000 a year as a project manager. He drove a luxury car, lived in a high-end apartment, and dressed the part. On the surface, he looked financially secure, but every major application told a different story. He was denied for high-limit cards, personal loans, and 0% offers. His issue was not income. It was structure.

His profile showed 72% utilization, three maxed-out cards, five inquiries within 90 days, and no primary card above a $1,500 limit. To the bank, this translated into a simple conclusion: high spending, low discipline, high risk.

Once Jason reduced utilization, allowed inquiries to age, closed subprime accounts, and rebuilt with higher-quality limits, access followed. Within nine months, he held multiple five-figure approvals across major banks. His income never changed. His behavior did.

Stage 1 rewards discipline, not lifestyle.

Stage 2: Relationship-Based Funding

(The Secret Step)

This is where real leverage begins. At Stage 2, banks stop treating you like a stranger and begin treating you like a potential partner. Credit decisions expand beyond your report and into your relationship with the institution.

At this level, approvals are influenced by:

- deposit behavior
- length of relationship
- internal risk score
- overdraft frequency
- account usage patterns
- volume and consistency of cash flow

These internal bank scores are not your FICO. They are proprietary risk assessments built from daily interaction with your accounts.

A strong internal score is shaped by:

- debit transactions
- deposit consistency
- average balances
- account age
- overdraft activity

- login frequency
- overall relationship history

When this internal profile is strong, banks extend access more easily, even when your FICO is not perfect. This is why someone with a 690 score may receive $30,000 approvals while another person with a 750 score is denied.

The principle behind this stage is simple but rarely taught.

Billionaire Principle #1:

Banks invest in relationships, not numbers.

To build relationship-based funding, you must behave like a long-term client:

✔ Open checking and savings accounts with banks you want funding from

✔ Deposit money weekly, even in small amounts

✔ Maintain stable average balances

✔ Avoid overdrafts entirely

✔ Use debit cards occasionally to show activity

✔ Wait at least 90 days before applying for credit

When these conditions are met, banks begin offering overdraft lines, personal loans, pre-approvals, credit line increases, and eventually business products.

Once relationship trust is established, you are ready for Stage 3.

Stage 3: Business Credit Leverage

(Your Second Identity)

An LLC is not a business. It is a vessel. A container for capital, a shell for liability, and a legal double for funding. When structured correctly, it becomes a second financial identity.

At this stage, you stop viewing your LLC as paperwork and begin treating it as a parallel version of yourself, complete with its own identity, limits, and growth trajectory. You are no longer building one credit profile. You are building two.

This is where leverage accelerates. Business credit limits grow ten to twenty times faster than personal limits because banks expect businesses to spend aggressively. What looks risky for an individual appears normal for an entity.

That is why personal cards often cap out between $25,000 and $50,000, while business cards can scale into six figures and beyond. Your personal score opens the door. Your business profile escorts you into the vault.

To grow business credit effectively, several rules must be followed:

The 7 Rules of Business Credit Growth

1. Your business address must look credible.
   Use a virtual office or commercial address, not a residence.

2. Your business phone number must be a dedicated business line.
   Banks verify this digitally.

3. Your domain and email must match your business name.
   Avoid free email providers.

4. Your NAICS code determines your risk classification.
   High-risk industries receive lower limits.

5. Your business must maintain its own checking account.
   Preferably with a major institution.

6. Your business needs consistent deposits.
   Small, steady deposits matter more than sporadic spikes.

7. Your personal score controls early approvals.
   Over time, the business becomes self-powered.

When these systems are aligned, funding accelerates.

Story: The Woman Who 10×'d Her Funding Using Only Her LLC

Monique ran a hair-braiding business entirely in cash. She had no receipts, no merchant deposits, and no formal structure. Once she incorporated, opened a business account, deposited income properly, selected a clean NAICS code, and waited 90 days, access followed.

Her initial approvals totaled under $40,000. Within months, credit line increases and new approvals pushed her total business funding past $86,000. She didn't change industries. She changed systems.

Stage 4: Capital Scaling

(From $50k to $500k)

Once both personal and business profiles are aligned, capital becomes multiplicative. At this stage, wealthy families use credit to acquire assets that generate cashflow, not expenses that create drag.

This is where funding supports:

- real estate portfolios
- car rental fleets
- high-cashflow businesses
- e-commerce brands
- consulting agencies
- logistics and transportation companies
- credit stacking strategies
- passive income systems

At this level, you possess personal credit, business credit, bank relationships, merchant history, and institutional trust. The funding ladder becomes exponential rather than linear.

This chapter sets the framework. The chapters ahead will break down each rung in detail.

7

FUNDING LADDER BREAKDOWN — MOVING FROM SMALL APPROVALS TO $100K–$500K

The Funding Ladder is one of the most misunderstood concepts in credit. Most people assume funding works in a straight line: fix your score, apply everywhere, and hope something sticks. That approach produces denials, wasted inquiries, low limits, and account shutdowns. Worse, it trains the system to see desperation rather than strategy.

Wealthy families never apply randomly. They move through banks in a precise sequence, allowing each approval to strengthen the next. The Funding Ladder exists because banks trust in layers, not leaps.

The ladder is governed by five core principles:

✓ **Principle 1: Trust Is Built in Stages**

No bank gives top-tier access to an unproven profile. Each approval earns the next one.

✓ **Principle 2: Limits Create Social Proof**

Banks are more comfortable extending credit when other banks already have.

✓ **Principle 3: Banks Copy Each Other**

One strong approval often triggers others.

✓ **Principle 4: Personal and Business Credit Must Be Cycled**

Alternating between the two multiplies access.

✓ Principle 5: Inquiries Must Be Clustered Intentionally

Scattered applications signal confusion. Strategic clustering signals competence.

With those principles in place, the ladder itself becomes clear.

The Four Tiers of the Funding Ladder

Every major lender fits into one of four tiers. Climbing them in order is not optional. Skipping tiers leads to rejection.

Tier 1 — The Relationship Builders

(Where You Start)

Tier 1 banks are designed to warm up your profile. They offer predictable underwriting, soft-pull pre-approvals, and forgiving limits. Their role is not to make you rich. Their role is to establish trust.

Common Tier 1 lenders include:

• Discover
• Capital One
• Apple Card (Goldman Sachs)
• Credit unions (local or national)

Tier 1 outcomes typically include:

• $1,000–$5,000 approvals
• early revolving credit
• primary tradelines
• your first real internal bank scores

Target outcome:
✓ 2–3 approvals
✓ $5K–$12K in total limits
✓ 30–45 days of clean reporting

Once these accounts are active and stable, your risk profile improves.

Tier 2 — The Mid-Level Banks

(The First Real Jump)

Tier 2 is where funding begins to feel meaningful. These banks are stricter, but they reward clean profiles, low utilization, and existing limits.

Tier 2 banks include:

- Bank of America
- Wells Fargo
- U.S. Bank
- Truist
- Regions
- KeyBank

At this level, banks look for proof that Tier 1 worked. They want to see that you didn't max out new cards or behave erratically.

Target outcome:

✓ 2–3 approvals

✓ $15K–$40K in combined limits

✓ your first $8K–$15K single card

✓ access to personal loans and lines of credit

Once Tier 2 is secured, Tier 3 becomes attainable.

Tier 3 — The Big Players

(Where Real Money Enters the Room)

Tier 3 banks represent the elite layer of personal credit. These institutions require clean profiles, disciplined usage, and restraint with inquiries.

Tier 3 banks include:

• Chase
• American Express
• Citi
• Barclays

This tier is where borrowers move into the $20K–$50K total personal limit range. It is also where soft-pull credit line increases become available and ecosystems begin to open.

Target outcome:

✔ $20K–$50K in personal limits

✔ eligibility for Amex credit line increases

✔ Chase and Citi ecosystem access

Tier 3 is not the endgame. It is the bridge.

Tier 4 — Business Funding

(The Vault Opens)

Tier 4 is where capital scaling begins. Business cards and lines of credit do not report to personal utilization and can be stacked strategically.

Tier 4 lenders include:

• American Express Business

• Chase Ink

• Citi Business

• Bank of America Business

• Navy Federal Business

• U.S. Bank Business

At this tier, funding can scale rapidly:
- $50K
- $100K
- $250K
- $500K+

Business funding is designed for expansion. Used correctly, it becomes the engine of asset acquisition rather than a source of personal debt.

The Actual Funding Sequence

(How the Ladder Is Climbed)

This is the order disciplined borrowers follow:

Step 1: Tier 1 Warm-Up
Secure 2–3 foundational approvals and establish usage.

Step 2: Tier 2 Expansion
Add mid-level banks once utilization and inquiries are controlled.

Step 3: Tier 3 Entry
Apply to elite lenders once your profile signals stability.

Step 4: Tier 4 Business Funding
Leverage your personal profile to unlock high-limit business access.

Each step strengthens the next. Skipping steps weakens the entire structure.

The Visual Summary

Personal Credit (Trust Building):
Tier 1 → Tier 2 → Tier 3

Business Credit (Capital Scaling):
Tier 4 → stacking → line increases → lines of credit → loans

Why the Funding Ladder Works

The ladder succeeds because it mirrors how banks think. It respects risk tolerance, rewards predictability, and converts discipline into leverage. When followed correctly, funding stops feeling random and starts feeling inevitable.

This chapter explains *how* access is sequenced. The next chapter explains *why* limits appear where they do and how to intentionally trigger higher approvals.

8

THE SECRET FORMULA FOR HIGH-LIMIT APPROVALS

Most people believe credit limits are based on income, credit score, or luck. They assume that higher earnings automatically lead to higher approvals, or that a strong score guarantees generous limits. That belief keeps them confused when approvals don't match expectations.

In reality, high credit limits are driven by psychology and pattern recognition. Banks extend larger limits to borrowers who have already demonstrated the ability to manage them. The system is not trying to reward ambition. It is trying to minimize risk.

This principle is known as **limit mirroring**. Banks feel safest giving you what looks familiar.

If your highest limit is $2,500, a $10,000 approval feels reckless to an underwriter. If your highest limit is $15,000, a $12,000 approval feels reasonable. The system does not ask what you want. It asks what you have already proven you can handle.

High-limit approvals are triggered by a specific combination of signals. When these signals align, limits rise quickly and predictably.

The 7 Factors That Trigger High Limits

Factor 1: Your Existing Highest Limit

Your current highest credit limit acts as a blueprint for future approvals. Banks mirror what already exists.
- $2,500 highest limit → $3,000–$5,000 approvals
- $12,000 highest limit → $10,000–$15,000 approvals
- $25,000 highest limit → $20,000–$30,000 approvals

This is why strategic limit growth matters more than the number of cards you hold.

Factor 2: Utilization Behavior

Banks don't just look at limits. They look at how you use them. High limits are extended to borrowers who demonstrate restraint.

The strongest profiles show:
- low reported utilization
- balances paid before due dates
- multiple payments per month
- no pattern of carrying heavy balances

High limits follow calm usage, not constant borrowing.

Factor 3: Inquiry Pattern

Inquiries tell a story. Random inquiries signal confusion or desperation. Clustered inquiries signal intent and strategy.

High-limit approvals are more likely when applications are grouped deliberately within short windows rather than scattered across months.

Factor 4: Deposit History and Internal Bank Scores

Internal bank scores quietly influence approvals more than most consumers realize. Consistent deposits, stable balances, and clean account management signal profitability.

Banks ask a simple question: *Has this person been good to us?*

When the answer is yes, approvals become easier, even if your external score is not perfect.

Factor 5: Age of Accounts

Time matters. Profiles with an average age of three or more years signal stability. Newer profiles feel unpredictable.

Authorized user tradelines, when added carefully from strong profiles, can accelerate perceived age without harming integrity.

Factor 6: Credit Mix

Strong profiles include a mix of revolving and installment accounts. This shows the system you can manage different forms of obligation without friction.

A single well-managed installment loan can meaningfully improve approval odds.

Factor 7: Payment Pattern

Elite borrowers behave predictably. They pay early, pay often, and rarely carry balances forward.

From the system's perspective, this behavior reduces uncertainty. Reduced uncertainty invites larger limits.

What This Chapter Really Teaches

High limits are not granted because you ask for them. They appear when your profile signals readiness. When the seven factors align, approvals feel almost automatic.

This is why two people with the same income and similar scores can receive dramatically different outcomes. One profile communicates discipline. The other communicates risk.

Once you understand this formula, you stop chasing limits and start *attracting* them. Your behavior does the negotiating for you.

The next chapter moves from theory into lender-specific reality. Different banks apply these principles differently, and knowing their internal rules allows you to apply pressure in the right places.

9

AMEX, CHASE, CITI & BANK SECRET RULES

Once you understand how high-limit approvals are triggered, the next advantage comes from knowing how individual banks interpret those signals. All major lenders evaluate risk differently. They share data, but they do not share philosophy. Treating them as interchangeable is one of the fastest ways to get denied.

This chapter breaks down the internal tendencies of the most powerful banks in the system. These are not myths or marketing promises. They are behavioral patterns banks reveal through consistent approval and denial outcomes. Banks operate within internal risk systems that track behavior long before an application is approved or denied.

American Express (AMEX)

American Express does not think in limits the way other banks do. Long term, it cares less about the number attached to your account and more about how you behave once access is granted.

Amex evaluates:

- spending patterns

- payment speed

- internal trust score

- relationship longevity

Because of this, Amex often extends one approval per hard pull and occasionally two. Charge cards such as Gold and Platinum have no preset spending limit, which allows Amex to dynamically assess risk based on behavior rather than static caps.

Key Amex rules include:

- eligibility for a 3× credit line increase after 90 days

- preference for fast payoffs and high spend

- strong bias toward business customers

- tendency to mirror your highest external limit

- internal reviews based on recent usage, not just history

Amex rewards borrowers who move confidently and pay decisively. If you hesitate or carry balances unnecessarily, growth slows. If you demonstrate control, limits expand rapidly.

Chase

Chase is protective of its ecosystem and enforces some of the strictest entry rules in consumer credit. It values cleanliness, patience, and long-term relationships.

Chase's most important policies include:

- the 5/24 rule, which automatically denies applicants who have opened five or more cards from any bank within 24 months

- preference for clean credit history with minimal recent derogatories

- strong weighting of checking and savings relationships

- soft-pull pre-approvals available in-branch for qualified clients

- high internal risk scoring

One of Chase's most powerful advantages is that its business cards generally do not report to personal credit utilization. This makes Chase a cornerstone for scaling without damaging personal profiles.

Chase does not reward urgency. It rewards restraint.

Citi

Citi is generous with limits but unforgiving with recent instability. It responds well to clean profiles and low utilization but reacts negatively to excessive inquiries or recent late payments.

Citi's internal tendencies include:

- preference for fewer than three inquiries within six months

- emphasis on revolving account history

- intolerance for recent delinquencies

- strong response to low utilization ratios

Citi is often best approached after Tier 2 and Tier 3 stability has been established. When timed correctly, it can deliver meaningful limits quickly.

Bank of America

Bank of America is relationship-driven to its core. More than many lenders, it weighs internal behavior heavily when deciding limits and approvals.

Bank of America values:

- consistent deposits

- stable balances

- long-term account history

- low-risk transactional behavior

Clients with strong banking relationships often receive higher limits and faster increases than their external profile alone would suggest. For this reason, Bank of America rewards patience more than optimization tricks.

How to Use This Information Strategically

The purpose of this chapter is not to memorize rules. It is to apply pressure where each bank is most responsive.

- Use Amex to scale quickly through behavior-based increases.

- Use Chase for ecosystem strength and business credit insulation.

- Use Citi for strategic mid-to-high limit jumps once stability is proven.

- Use Bank of America for relationship-driven expansion over time.

When you align your applications with each bank's internal logic, approvals stop feeling random. You stop applying emotionally and start applying surgically.

The system does not resist knowledgeable borrowers. It accommodates them.

10

BUSINESS CREDIT STACKING — $50K TO $250K IN 90 DAYS

Most people build business credit slowly because they follow an outdated model. They start with net-30 vendors, wait months for small starter accounts, and inch forward one approval at a time. That method was designed for a pre-fintech world and corporate timelines, not for modern entrepreneurs who understand leverage.

Wealthy operators use a different system: **business credit stacking**. This is the strategic acquisition of multiple high-limit business credit lines within a compressed window, using personal credit strength, business legitimacy, and inquiry timing to accelerate access without destroying the personal profile.

Business stacking is not reckless. It is calculated, and when done correctly, it allows borrowers to move from zero funding to meaningful capital in a matter of months rather than years.

The Psychology Behind Business Approvals

Banks approve business credit based on three overlapping evaluations. All three must align.

✓ **Personal Credit (Risk Backbone)**
Banks assess whether the owner is trustworthy. Your personal profile opens the door.

✓ **Business Structure (Legitimacy Blueprint)**
Banks ask whether the business looks real, stable, and scalable.

✓ **Banking Relationship (Internal Trust)**

Banks evaluate how you have already behaved inside their ecosystem.

When these elements are aligned, approvals often occur back-to-back. Banks are not collaborating, but they are competing for future transaction volume. The first approval signals opportunity to the rest.

The 9 Requirements for Business Credit Stacking

Before applying for a single business card, your entity must be structured correctly. This is non-negotiable.

✔ 1. A Legitimate Business Name
Avoid high-risk or flagged industries such as credit repair, finance, crypto, or cannabis. General professional services receive higher approvals.

✔ 2. A Professional Business Address
Use a virtual office, commercial address, or co-working space. Never use a residential address.

✔ 3. A Dedicated Business Phone Number
Use verified systems such as Google Voice, Grasshopper, or RingCentral.

✔ 4. A Business Domain and Matching Email
Avoid free email providers. Use a domain-based address aligned with your business name.

✔ 5. An EIN
Issued directly from the IRS.

✔ 6. A Proper NAICS Code
Low-risk industries receive higher limits and better terms.

✔ 7. A Business Checking Account
Preferably with a major national or strong regional bank.

✔ 8. Proof of Revenue
Consistency matters more than size. Predictable deposits outperform sporadic spikes.

✔ 9. A Clean Personal Profile

Typically a 700+ score, low utilization, limited inquiries, and no recent derogatories.

Once these nine elements are in place, stacking becomes possible.

The Business Credit Stacking Method

(The Exact Sequence)

Business stacking works because of sequencing, not volume. The order matters.

STEP 1: Soft-Pull Business Approvals

Begin with lenders that approve without a hard personal inquiry.

Common examples include:
* American Express business cards
* Capital on Tap
* Brex
* Divvy
* Ramp
* Stripe Capital (revenue-based)

These accounts establish early business activity without damaging personal utilization.

Expected range: $10K–$40K

STEP 2: Primary Bank Applications

(Hard Pull)

Next, apply with the bank where you already maintain business deposits. Internal trust significantly increases approval odds. Target products include:

* business cash cards

* unsecured business lines

* entry-level business loans

Expected range: $5K–$25K

STEP 3: Major Business Cards

(The Heavy Hitters)

Once early approvals are secured, move into high-limit business cards. Common targets include:

- Amex Business Gold
- Amex Business Blue
- Chase Ink Preferred or Cash
- CitiBusiness AAdvantage
- Bank of America Business Cash
- U.S. Bank Business Leverage

This step alone often produces the largest jumps.

Expected range: $40K–$120K

STEP 4: Secondary Banks

(Additional Stack)

Regional and secondary banks frequently approve back-to-back once major cards are secured. Examples include:

- PNC
- KeyBank
- Regions
- Fifth Third
- Huntington

Expected range: $20K–$50K

STEP 5: Business Lines of Credit and Loans

With multiple strong accounts reporting, banks begin offering unsecured lines of credit and term loans.

Typical ranges include:

- $25K–$50K lines
- $10K–$30K term loans

This pushes total access into six-figure territory.

The 90-Day Stacking Calendar

Days 1–30:
Structuring, account setup, and soft-pull approvals
Expected funding: $10K–$40K

Days 30–60:
Primary bank and major card applications
Expected funding: $40K–$120K

Days 60–90:
Secondary banks and lines of credit
Expected funding: $20K–$60K

The 5 Rules of Successful Stacking

✓ **Cluster inquiries intentionally**
Apply within 5–14 day windows.

✓ **Always apply business first**
Business credit does not report to personal utilization.

✓ **Never max new business cards**
Keep utilization under 25–40% initially.

✓ **Never lie about revenue**
Banks verify through deposits and patterns.

✓ **Use funding for assets, not lifestyle**
Leverage must produce cashflow.

What This Chapter Really Teaches

Business credit stacking is not about speed for its own sake. It is about alignment. When structure, behavior, and timing work together, access expands naturally. Stacking is how people move from approval to ownership. From access to control.

The next chapter takes that access and turns it into systems that generate income.

11

THE MILLION-DOLLAR PLAY — TURNING CREDIT INTO CASHFLOW

Credit only becomes powerful when it produces income. Until then, it is just potential. The mistake most people make at this stage is assuming that access itself equals wealth. It does not. Access is neutral. What matters is what you deploy it into.

Wealthy families treat credit as seed capital, not spending power. They move money once, then let systems move it again and again. This chapter explains how capital is converted into cashflow deliberately, repeatably, and without emotional decision-making. Capital allocation systems reward stability, documentation, and predictability. They punish volatility, emotion, and inconsistency.

The goal is not to look rich. The goal is to become independent of constant labor.

The Three Rules of the Million-Dollar Play

Before discussing specific strategies, three rules govern every successful deployment of credit.

✔ **Rule 1: Credit Must Buy Assets, Not Appearances**
If credit does not return money, time, or leverage, it is being misused.

✔ **Rule 2: Cashflow Comes Before Appreciation**
Speculation follows stability, not the other way around.

✔ **Rule 3: Systems Beat Hustle**

Anything that depends on constant personal effort will eventually collapse.

Every strategy in this chapter obeys these rules.

The Five Asset Classes That Convert Credit Into Cashflow

Not all investments work well with credit. The wealthy focus on assets that generate predictable returns quickly enough to service debt while still producing profit.

The most commonly used asset classes include:

• cashflow real estate

• vehicle-based businesses

• service businesses with low overhead

• digital or automated platforms

• contract-based operations

Each has advantages. The key is matching the asset to your risk tolerance, skill set, and available capital.

Play #1: Cashflow Real Estate

(Rent Pays the Note)

Real estate becomes powerful when rent exceeds debt service. Wealthy investors use credit to acquire income-producing properties where tenants pay the loan, taxes, insurance, and maintenance.

Common entry points include:

• short-term rentals

• mid-term furnished housing

• small multifamily properties

• house hacking strategies

The objective is not ownership for ego. It is ownership that removes personal expense from the equation.

Play #2: Vehicle-Based Businesses

(Assets That Move)

Vehicles are depreciating assets, but businesses that use vehicles can be highly profitable when structured correctly.

Examples include:

• car rental operations

• box truck logistics

• medical courier services

• mobile service businesses

Credit is used to acquire vehicles. Contracts or rentals produce cashflow. Revenue services the debt and funds expansion.

Play #3: Service Businesses

(Low Overhead, High Margins)

Service businesses scale quickly when demand is consistent and delivery is systemized.

Strong candidates include:

• consulting agencies

• marketing services

• cleaning or maintenance companies

• staffing and placement firms

Credit funds startup costs, marketing, and payroll float. Once contracts are secured, cashflow becomes predictable.

Play #4: Digital & Automated Platforms

(Leverage Without Location)

Digital businesses allow scale without physical assets. While riskier, they offer high margins when executed properly.

Examples include:

• e-commerce brands

• subscription platforms

• SaaS or digital products

• content-driven revenue models

Credit supports inventory, advertising, or development. Systems, not constant attention, drive returns.

Play #5: Contract-Based Operations

(Predictability Wins)

Contracts reduce uncertainty. When revenue is locked in, credit becomes safer to deploy.

Common models include:

• government or municipal contracts

• long-term service agreements

• B2B supply contracts

• franchise-style licensing

Banks favor these models because income is documented and reliable.

The Million-Dollar Loop

(How Wealth Compounds)

This is the pattern wealthy families repeat:

1. Use credit to acquire an asset

2. Use the asset to generate cashflow

3. Use cashflow to pay debt and build reserves

4. Use reserves and equity to acquire the next asset

5. Repeat without increasing personal risk

Over time, the individual becomes optional. The systems remain.

Why Most People Fail at This Stage

Failure here is rarely technical. It is psychological.

People misuse credit because they want relief, validation, or comfort. They chase fast wins instead of durable systems. They deploy capital emotionally instead of strategically.

The wealthy delay gratification not because they enjoy sacrifice, but because they understand momentum.

What This Chapter Unlocks

This chapter marks a turning point. You now understand how credit becomes income, how income becomes freedom, and how systems replace hustle.

The next chapter moves beyond money entirely. It addresses the identity required to hold this level of access without collapsing under pressure.

12

THE FUNDING-TO-WEALTH FORMULA

Wealthy people do not use credit randomly. They follow a repeatable sequence that turns access into ownership over time. When this sequence is respected, credit becomes a tool for liberation. When it is ignored, credit becomes a trap.

The formula is simple, but it is not accidental:

Credit → Capital → Cashflow → Leverage → Asset →

Equity → Wealth

Each stage builds on the one before it. Skip a step and the system collapses. Respect the order and momentum compounds.

Most people follow a very different path, often without realizing it:

Credit → Lifestyle → Debt

The difference between these two paths is not intelligence or effort. It is understanding how leverage is supposed to work.

Credit is not wealth. It is permission. Capital is what happens when that permission is converted into usable funds. Cashflow is what happens when those funds are deployed into something that produces income. Leverage follows naturally when income can support more access. Assets are acquired when leverage is used intentionally. Equity accumulates when assets are held rather than consumed. Wealth is simply the long-term result of repeating this cycle without breaking it.

This is why people with access but no structure feel busy but remain stuck, while others with modest beginnings quietly scale.

To see how the formula works in real life, consider Kenya's story.

Story: From $14 an Hour to Five Properties in 18 Months

Kenya worked as a CNA earning $14 an hour. She was exhausted, overworked, and constantly behind on bills. Nothing about her situation looked like wealth in progress. What she lacked was not discipline or intelligence. It was leverage.

Once her credit profile was repaired and aligned, she followed the Funding Ladder exactly as designed:

- Tier 1 → Tier 2 → Tier 3 → Tier 4

- stacked approximately $96,000 in business credit

- used an American Express line to furnish two Airbnb units

- used a Chase Ink card to fund a vending route

- used a Bank of America Business Advantage card for a duplex down payment

Each move followed the formula. Credit became capital. Capital created cashflow. Cashflow supported leverage. Leverage acquired assets. Assets built equity.

Today, Kenya owns:
- two Airbnbs
- one duplex
- two vending routes

Her monthly cashflow exceeds $8,200. She did not become smarter. She did not earn a new degree. She did not stumble into luck. She learned how to use credit the way wealthy families do: as a bridge, not a reward.

Why This Formula Works

The Funding-to-Wealth Formula succeeds because it respects how systems respond to behavior. Banks extend more access when existing obligations are serviced calmly. Assets grow when income exceeds expense. Equity compounds when assets are held through cycles rather than flipped emotionally.

The system rewards consistency, not excitement.

This is also why misuse of credit is so destructive. When credit is spent on lifestyle instead of infrastructure, there is no cashflow to stabilize it. Without stabilization, leverage becomes pressure. Pressure leads to bad decisions, and bad decisions lead to collapse.

Wealth is not created by how much credit you obtain. It is created by how well you convert that credit into structures that pay you back.

What This Chapter Closes

This chapter completes the work of **Part III**. You now understand how repaired credit becomes funding, how funding becomes cashflow, and how cashflow becomes equity and wealth. The ladder is no longer theoretical. It is proven.

But access and assets introduce a new challenge: sustainability.

In the next Part, the focus shifts away from tactics and toward identity. Holding power requires a different internal structure than acquiring it. Without that structure, everything built here can be lost just as quickly as it was gained.

PART IV

BECOMING FINANCIALLY UNTOUCHABLE

13

THE IDENTITY SHIFT — FROM CONSUMER TO KONTROLLER

Most people move through the world as consumers, reacting to their financial reality instead of shaping it. Their decisions are driven by emotion, urgency, fear, and the need for approval. They chase rewards they do not fully understand, avoid institutions that could empower them, and hide from mistakes instead of learning from them. Even when opportunity is present, they hesitate, waiting for permission rather than positioning themselves to act.

This pattern is not a reflection of intelligence or effort. It is a reflection of identity. When your internal framework is unstable, your external results will mirror that instability. Money flows in, then flows out. Opportunities appear, then disappear. Nothing anchors, nothing compounds, and nothing builds.

A KONTROLLER moves differently because their identity is different.

Where the consumer reacts, the KONTROLLER prepares. Where the consumer moves emotionally, the KONTROLLER moves with precision. They use debt deliberately, converting credit into leverage rather than consumption. They do not see banks as obstacles, but as structured institutions governed by rules, which can be understood, anticipated, and used. Instead of waiting for approval, they position themselves for selection, acting with clarity and refining as they go. Their decisions are not governed by panic or impulse, but by discipline and ownership of outcomes.

What separates these two ways of moving is not income, background, or access. It is identity.

Identity functions as an operating system. It determines how you interpret pressure, how you respond to risk, and how you make decisions when money is involved. If your identity is reactive, your financial life will be reactive. If your identity is structured, your financial life will begin to stabilize and expand. When identity shifts, behavior changes. When behavior changes, outcomes begin to compound.

The Three Financial Identities

Every person operates from one of three dominant financial identities. These are not labels of worth, but patterns of behavior that produce predictable results.

Identity 1 — The Consumer

The consumer's relationship with money is emotional and reactive. Their decisions are shaped by immediate needs, internal discomfort, and external pressure. They spend to feel better, borrow to maintain appearances, and respond to financial situations without a long-term framework.

Consumers may earn a high income or a low one, but the pattern remains the same: money passes through them without creating lasting change. Their behavior does not compound because it is inconsistent, and inconsistency prevents stability.

Their decisions are often driven by:
- comfort
- fear
- urgency
- desire
- insecurity
- validation

As long as identity remains rooted in consumption, financial progress will remain temporary.

Identity 2 — The Operator

The operator introduces discipline. They pay bills on time, manage obligations responsibly, and avoid unnecessary risk. Their financial life is structured, predictable, and stable. They understand the importance of consistency and have developed habits that protect what they earn.

However, stability alone does not produce scale.

Operators manage money well, but they do not command the systems that multiply it. They preserve resources, but they rarely expand them. Their focus is on maintaining order rather than creating leverage, which keeps them safe but limits their growth.

Operators are defined by:
- consistency
- responsibility
- risk awareness
- structured habits
- financial stability

They build a strong foundation, but without a shift in identity, that foundation does not evolve into expansion.

Identity 3 — The KONTROLLER

The KONTROLLER operates from a fundamentally different framework. They understand that financial systems are governed by behavior, patterns, and predictability, and they align themselves accordingly. Money is not viewed as currency alone, but as influence. Credit is not viewed as a score, but as controlled leverage. Banks are not seen as threats, but as institutions that respond to disciplined behavior.

A KONTROLLER approaches assets with intention. Assets are not symbols of success; they are instruments of control that expand reach, autonomy, and long-term positioning. Risk is not avoided or feared, but measured, structured, and used strategically.

This is why KONTROLLERS tend to build and control:
- real estate
- land

- companies
- cashflow
- networks
- influence
- time

They do not wait for permission to act. They position themselves so that opportunities recognize them. Their consistency creates trust, and that trust becomes access.

At this level, financial outcomes are no longer driven by effort alone, but by alignment. Banks and institutions do not reward intention; they respond to predictable behavior. Systems open to individuals who demonstrate stability under pressure, discipline over time, and clarity in decision-making.

Wealth rarely collapses from a lack of opportunity. It collapses from instability.

When identity is structured, behavior stabilizes. When behavior stabilizes, systems begin to respond. Access expands not because it is requested, but because it is earned through consistency.

This book was not written to make you a better consumer or a more organized operator. It was written to guide you into a different identity, one that creates stability before opportunity, discipline before access, and structure before scale.

However, even this is not the final stage. There is a level beyond control.

The Bridge — Ascension Into Sovereignty

Understanding consumers, operators, and KONTROLLERS reveals the architecture of financial behavior. It explains why some people remain reactive, why others achieve stability, and why a small group gains access and multiplies it.

Beyond control lies a higher level of positioning.

At this level, the individual is no longer simply navigating systems. They are shaping the environments those systems respond to. Their presence carries weight. Their decisions influence direction. Their structure extends beyond personal discipline into something that affects outcomes at scale.

This is not a shift in tactics. It is a shift in classification.

It requires a level of internal stability that does not fracture under pressure, a clarity that is not disrupted by noise, and a consistency that remains intact regardless of circumstance.

Very few reach this level, not because it is inaccessible, but because it requires a depth of internal structure most people never develop.

This is where control evolves into command, and this is where the next chapter begins.

14

THE KONTROLLER — THE RULES OF SUPREME POWER

A KONTROLLER moves in a way that is not easily recognized at first glance. They are not louder, faster, or more aggressive than everyone else in the room. Instead, they are precise. While others react to pressure, they remain steady. While others rush or hesitate, they act with intention. Their presence is not defined by noise, but by consistency. In moments of chaos, they become the still point others unconsciously organize around.

This difference is not personality. It is structure.

A KONTROLLER is not unaffected by pressure because life is easy. They are unaffected because they have engineered themselves to withstand pressure without losing clarity. Their responses are not dictated by emotion, urgency, or external validation. They are governed by internal discipline, which allows them to remain consistent whether conditions are favorable or uncertain. This is what separates those who gain access from those who sustain and expand it.

KONTROLLER Defined

A KONTROLLER is defined by an internal architecture that does not collapse under stress. They regulate their emotional state, maintain clarity in uncertainty, and make decisions based on structure rather than reaction. Their behavior remains predictable, even in unpredictable environments, which is why systems begin to trust them over time.

This identity is characterized by:

- disciplined decision-making
- stability under pressure
- precision in the use of leverage
- consistency across changing conditions
- clarity in complex situations
- the ability to generate and sustain opportunity

Their outcomes are not accidental. They are the result of repeated, structured behavior that compounds.

At the core of this identity is one defining trait: stability under pressure.

Most people become inconsistent when circumstances change. They overreact during downturns, hesitate during opportunity, and shift direction based on emotion. A KONTROLLER does the opposite. Their behavior remains steady regardless of external conditions. They do not collapse under pressure; they refine within it. They do not become reactive when situations intensify; they become more precise.

This consistency is what systems respond to. Banks, institutions, and markets are not influenced by intention or potential. They respond to patterns. When behavior remains stable over time, trust is established. When trust is established, access expands. The KONTROLLER understands that pressure is not an obstacle to avoid, but a condition that reveals whether their structure is strong enough to sustain growth.

KONTROLLER Laws— The Structural Rules of Power

The principles that govern this identity are not motivational ideas. They are structural rules that reinforce consistency. They exist to eliminate emotional decision-making and replace it with disciplined behavior. Without structure, identity fragments under pressure. With structure, identity stabilizes and compounds.

The following laws define how a KONTROLLER maintains that structure.

LAW 1 — Become the Source, Not the Seeker

A KONTROLLER does not chase money, attention, or validation. They develop internal stability and clarity that positions them to be selected rather than overlooked. When presence is grounded and behavior is consistent, opportunities begin to align naturally.

Stability attracts capital because it signals reliability. When you become the source, you shift from asking for access to being recognized as someone who can handle it.

LAW 2 — You Cannot Be Emotional With Money

Emotion introduces instability into financial decision-making. When decisions are driven by fear, urgency, or excitement, consistency breaks and outcomes become unpredictable.

A KONTROLLER feels emotion but does not act from it. Money responds to disciplined logic and structured behavior. When emotion is removed from execution, decision-making becomes clear and repeatable.

LAW 3 — Wealth Requires Detachment

Attachment to outcomes, opinions, and past mistakes creates fragility. Fragility leads to hesitation, overcorrection, and loss of control under pressure.

A KONTROLLER practices detachment by releasing:
- the need for approval
- fear of failure
- emotional attachment to past outcomes
- dependence on external validation

Detachment is not indifference. It is clarity that allows decisions to remain precise.

LAW 4 — Use Pressure as Fuel

Pressure is often misinterpreted as a signal to retreat. In reality, it is a signal that expansion is occurring. Growth introduces complexity, and complexity introduces pressure.

A KONTROLLER uses pressure as information. It reveals where refinement is needed and where strength already exists. Instead of resisting pressure, they use it to sharpen execution and improve structure.

LAW 5 — Leverage Is Your Birthright

Financial systems are designed to extend capital in exchange for predictable behavior. Without understanding this, leverage feels intimidating. With understanding, it becomes a tool.

A KONTROLLER studies how systems operate and positions themselves accordingly. As clarity increases, fear decreases. Leverage is no longer avoided; it is applied with intention.

LAW 6 — Move Like You Belong Everywhere

Confidence is not performance. It is alignment between identity and action. When uncertainty drives behavior, opportunities become inconsistent.

A KONTROLLER moves with certainty because their behavior is grounded in structure. Systems respond to that certainty. When you act as though you belong, and your behavior supports it, access begins to reflect that alignment.

LAW 7 — Your Name Is a Brand

Reputation functions as a form of capital. Over time, consistent behavior builds credibility, and credibility reduces resistance within systems.

A KONTROLLER treats their name as an asset by ensuring it represents:

- reliability
- discipline
- consistency

- trustworthiness

As credibility compounds, opportunities begin to appear without effort.

LAW 8 — Learn Faster Than You Spend

A lack of understanding leads to inefficient use of capital. Without clarity, money is deployed reactively rather than strategically.

A KONTROLLER prioritizes comprehension before execution. Knowledge allows capital to be applied with precision, which increases the likelihood of sustainable outcomes. Learning accelerates growth because it reduces costly mistakes.

LAW 9 — Never Let Comfort Seduce You

Comfort encourages stagnation. When growth slows, structure weakens, and opportunities diminish.

A KONTROLLER chooses challenge over ease and expansion over stability alone. Discomfort becomes a signal for growth rather than something to avoid. Consistent pressure maintains forward movement.

LAW 10 — Execute Before You Feel Ready

Waiting for certainty often results in inaction. Clarity rarely appears before movement; it develops through it.

A KONTROLLER acts with informed intention, then refines based on results. Execution creates feedback, and feedback creates improvement. Progress is driven by action, not hesitation.

LAW 11 — Protect Your Energy Like a Fortress

Energy is a limited resource that influences focus, decision-making, and execution. When it is depleted, performance declines.

A KONTROLLER protects their energy by managing:
1. time

2. attention
3. environment
4. relationships

Boundaries are not personal. They are strategic decisions that preserve capacity for high-level execution.

LAW 12 — Money Respects the Person Who Respects Themselves

Financial outcomes reflect internal standards. When discipline is low, inconsistency increases. When standards rise, behavior aligns accordingly.

A KONTROLLER maintains self-respect through structured habits, clear boundaries, and consistent execution. As internal standards improve, external results begin to reflect that change.

These laws are not meant to be memorized. They are meant to be lived.

A KONTROLLER is not defined by what they know, but by how consistently they apply it. Over time, these principles become embedded into behavior, and behavior becomes identity.

When identity stabilizes, results begin to compound. When results compound, access expands. Once access expands, the individual is no longer reacting to opportunity. They are positioned within it. This is what it means to operate with power.

From here forward, the book no longer teaches how to acquire. It teaches how to **hold, protect, and govern**.

15

THE SILENT LAWS OF FINANCIAL POWER

There are lessons the wealthy pass down quietly, often behind closed doors and within families. They are rarely taught in school, rarely spoken aloud in public, and almost never explained plainly. The middle class rarely hears them, and the poor often discover them only after time has already exacted its cost.

These are not motivational slogans. They are operating principles. They are the silent laws that govern how financial power is built, protected, and transferred.

Law 1 — Don't Work for Money. Make Money Work for You.

Money is not simply earned. It is controlled. Working for money trades time for income. Making money work multiplies time through systems.

The wealthy do not reject work. They reject dependency on labor alone. Their goal is not constant effort, but controlled return.

Law 2 — Never Use Personal Credit to Impress People

Using personal credit to impress others creates debt without leverage. It produces applause without equity.

Wealthy individuals use business credit to acquire assets that impress their banker, not their friends. Approval matters more than admiration. Access matters more than appearance.

Law 3 — Debt Is Only Dangerous to People without a Plan

Debt without purpose is poison. It drains resources and creates pressure. Debt with purpose is power. It accelerates outcomes when guided by structure and intention.

The difference is not the debt itself, but whether it serves a strategy.

Law 4 — Invest Early and Let Time Multiply You

Time is the strongest currency available. It compounds discipline, magnifies consistency, and rewards patience.

Those who delay investing are forced to rely on intensity later. Those who begin early allow time to do the heavy lifting.

Law 5 — Focus Beats Intelligence

You do not need to be the smartest person in the room. You need to be the most aligned.

Focus eliminates waste. Alignment removes friction. Intelligence without direction scatters energy. Focus applied consistently creates momentum.

Law 6 — Ownership Is the Only Path to Freedom

Freedom does not come from income alone. It comes from ownership.

Unfuckwithable people work toward owning:
- their time
- their assets
- their income streams
- their decisions
- their identity

Ownership is what separates participation from control.

Law 7 — Wealthy People Don't Save Money. They Store Value.

Saving preserves money. Storing value grows it. The wealthy understand the difference. They store value in:

- real estate
- businesses
- productive assets
- land
- intellectual property

Value storage protects wealth from erosion and positions it for growth.

Law 8 — You Must Expect Abundance

Scarcity thinking repels opportunity because it communicates fear. Abundance thinking attracts opportunity because it communicates readiness.

Expectation shapes behavior. Behavior shapes results. Wealth responds to those who expect capacity, not limitation.

Law 9 — Never Let Your Ambition Shrink to Fit Your Environment

Your environment either expands you or confines you. If it limits your thinking, your standards, or your expectations, it must be upgraded.

Wealthy individuals curate environments that stretch them. Comfort zones do not produce legacy.

Law 10 — You Are Your First Asset

Before investing in anything else, invest in yourself. That means investing in:

- your knowledge
- your discipline

- your psychology
- your habits
- your energy

Every external asset is limited by the internal one managing it. When you become stronger, everything you touch performs better. 82

Why These Laws Are Silent

These principles are rarely spoken aloud because they shift power. Once understood, they change how decisions are made, how risk is evaluated, and how systems are navigated.

This chapter reinforces what Part IV is teaching: wealth is not secured by access alone. It is secured by alignment, discipline, and quiet mastery.

16

THE FINAL EVOLUTION — BECOMING A FINANCIAL WEAPON

Every transformation reaches a moment where change is no longer something you practice. It becomes something you are. This is that moment.

Up to this point, you have learned how credit works, how access is built, how capital is deployed, and how power is protected. But the final evolution is not technical. It is internal. It is the point at which your behavior stabilizes because your identity has caught up with your capacity.

This is where most people never arrive.

The Difference Between Growth and Evolution

Growth is adding skills. Evolution is changing form.

People can grow financially without evolving psychologically, and when they do, collapse is almost guaranteed. Expansion without evolution creates pressure the nervous system cannot regulate. Evolution resolves that tension by reshaping how you move through risk, opportunity, and responsibility.

At this stage, you no longer need rules to behave correctly. The behavior is automatic.

The Signs of Final Evolution

Final evolution is quiet. It does not announce itself. It looks like:

- calm decision-making under stress

- reduced emotional reactivity

- disciplined use of leverage

- patience with long timelines

- comfort with delayed gratification

- consistency regardless of external noise

You are no longer impressed by speed. You are impressed by sustainability.

Power Without Performance

One of the clearest signs of evolution is that you stop performing wealth. You no longer need validation through appearance, spending, or explanation.

You do not talk about your plans prematurely. You do not overshare strategy. You move deliberately and let results speak.

This is not secrecy for ego. It is restraint for effectiveness.

The Moment Control Replaces Effort

Earlier in the journey, effort did most of the work. You pushed, learned, corrected, and repeated. In final evolution, control replaces effort.

Systems carry weight. Habits enforce discipline. Identity governs behavior. Decisions feel lighter because fewer of them are emotional.

You are no longer fighting yourself.

The Responsibility of Power

With evolution comes responsibility. Power magnifies impact, both positive and negative. Untouchable individuals understand that their decisions ripple outward through families, teams, and communities.

They become intentional about what they build, who they support, and what they refuse to participate in. Not because they are superior, but because they are accountable.

Why People Lose Access After They Gain It

The most dangerous moment in a financial journey is immediately after expansion. New limits create temptation. New income creates entitlement. New freedom creates false security.

Common self-sabotage patterns include:
- lifestyle expansion
- reckless leverage
- emotional spending
- blurred personal and business finances
- ignoring cash reserves
- chasing status instead of stability

None of these failings are technical. They are psychological.

The Untouchable Operating System

Financially untouchable people follow a different internal code. Their behavior is boring by design. They:
- maintain cash buffers
- keep utilization intentionally low
- stagger risk rather than stack it
- separate lifestyle from leverage
- reinvest before rewarding themselves

Boring behavior produces extraordinary outcomes

What Comes Next

This chapter closes **Part IV**. You are no longer being prepared to gain access or protect it. You are being prepared to extend it beyond yourself.

The next stage is not about who you become. It is about what you leave behind.

Part V: The Empire Blueprint begins here. This is where power becomes transferable, where systems outlive individuals, and where wealth is no longer measured by accumulation but by endurance.

You are no longer learning how to move through the world.

You are learning how to shape it.

PART V

THE EMPIRE BLUEPRINT

17

GENERATIONAL EMPIRE

Most people measure wealth by what they accumulate. Empires are measured by what they *outlast*.

A generational empire is not about excess or domination. It is about continuity. It is the ability to transfer power, opportunity, and protection across time without starting over every generation. What you are building now is not just for comfort. It is for permanence. This is the distinction between success and legacy.

At the highest level, systems are no longer transactional. They are institutional, designed to outlast individuals and regulate behavior across generations.

Why Most Wealth Dies in Three Generations

There is a reason the phrase exists. Wealth collapses when it is transferred without structure. Money alone does not survive inheritance. Systems do.

The first generation builds through effort and risk. The second enjoys access without context. The third inherits resources without discipline. Without education, identity, and governance, wealth erodes quietly and completely. A generational empire solves this by design.

Empire Is Built on Systems, Not Individuals

Individuals age. Systems endure.

Empires are constructed through repeatable frameworks that operate independently of any single person. They include legal structures, asset vehicles, operating rules, and cultural values that guide decision-making even when the founder is absent.

This is why wealthy families prioritize ownership over income and governance over lifestyle. They understand that systems, once built correctly, carry forward without constant intervention.

The Four Pillars of a Generational Empire

Every lasting empire rests on four foundational pillars.

Pillar 1: Ownership Structures

Assets must be owned in ways that protect them from fragmentation, taxation erosion, and mismanagement. Trusts, holding companies, and layered entities are not complexity for its own sake. They are continuity tools.

Pillar 2: Cashflow Engines

Empires do not rely on a single source of income. They operate multiple cashflow streams that stabilize one another across economic cycles. When one slows, another sustains.

Pillar 3: Governance and Rules

Clear rules prevent chaos. Governance defines who can decide, under what conditions, and with what accountability. This prevents emotional decision-making from destroying long-term assets.

Pillar 4: Cultural Transmission

Values must be taught, not assumed. Discipline, responsibility, and stewardship are passed down intentionally, or they disappear.

Wealth Without Identity Is a Liability

Money placed in the hands of individuals without identity becomes dangerous. It amplifies weakness instead of strength. This is why generational builders invest as heavily in education and character as they do in assets.

The goal is not to create heirs who consume. It is to cultivate stewards who expand.

Thinking Beyond a Single Lifetime

Generational thinkers plan in decades, not quarters. They ask different questions. Instead of "What can I buy?" they ask, "What can this support long after I'm gone?" Instead of "How much do I make?" they ask, "How does this protect the next generation?"

This shift changes everything from investment choices to business structures to daily behavior.

The Responsibility of Empire

Legacy-building is not about hiding from risk. It is about surviving it intact. When others pull back, you remain positioned. When others panic, you deploy capital calmly. This is how generational players win. They are still standing when cycles turn.

Building an empire carries weight. It means your decisions shape not just your life, but the lives of people who may never meet you. That responsibility demands restraint, foresight, and humility.

Empires are not loud. They are stable.

What This Chapter Opens

This chapter opens **Part V** by reframing wealth as something that must be designed to endure. The chapters that follow will show how empires multiply, how bloodlines are protected, and how names become institutions.

You are no longer building for yourself alone. You are building something that must survive you.

18

THE BLOODLINE PRINCIPLE — BUILDING WEALTH THAT OUTLIVES YOU

Most people misunderstand inheritance. They believe it begins with money and ends with distribution. In reality, inheritance begins with identity and ends with expectation. Money is only the most visible part of what gets passed down.

The Bloodline Principle states this simply: *what a family believes about itself determines what it is able to sustain.* Wealth follows belief, not the other way around.

Why Money Alone Fails Families

Money passed without structure becomes confusion. Children inherit resources without context, responsibility without preparation, and power without restraint. The result is not abundance. It is erosion.

Families that lose wealth across generations do not lack money. They lack continuity. They fail to pass down the rules, the reasoning, and the responsibility that made the money possible in the first place.

Bloodline Is Not Biology. It Is Conditioning.

A bloodline is not defined by DNA alone. It is defined by patterns. How a family talks about money. How it responds to risk. How it handles failure. How it teaches responsibility.

Families unknowingly train their bloodlines every day. Some teach fear, scarcity, and avoidance. Others teach stewardship, expectation, and authority.

The Bloodline Principle makes this intentional.

The Three Layers of Bloodline Transmission

Lasting families pass down more than assets. They transmit three essential layers.

Layer 1: Belief

Belief sets the ceiling. If children are taught that wealth is dangerous, undeserved, or temporary, they will unconsciously dismantle it. If they are taught that ownership is normal and responsibility is expected, they rise to it.

Layer 2: Systems

Systems provide rails. Trusts, entities, operating agreements, and clear decision frameworks prevent chaos. Systems remove guesswork and reduce emotional decision-making.

Layer 3: Standards

Standards govern behavior. They define what is acceptable, what is expected, and what is not tolerated. Standards are enforced through culture, not punishment.

Raising Stewards, Not Beneficiaries

Beneficiaries consume. Stewards protect, grow, and transfer.

Families who endure teach their children *why* assets exist before teaching them *how* to use them. Access is layered gradually, tied to maturity, responsibility, and contribution.

Nothing is automatic. Everything is earned through demonstrated alignment with family values.

The Role of Expectation

Expectation shapes performance. When children are raised knowing they are part of something larger than themselves, their decisions change. They act with awareness that their behavior reflects a lineage, not just an individual life.

This expectation is not pressure. It is grounding.

Breaking Destructive Cycles

The Bloodline Principle is also redemptive. It allows families to interrupt cycles of poverty, instability, and self-sabotage. One generation can change the trajectory permanently by redefining belief, installing systems, and enforcing standards.

This is how first-generation builders become founders of lasting dynasties.

What This Chapter Establishes

This chapter reframes inheritance as education, expectation, and structure rather than money alone. It teaches that bloodlines are built deliberately, not accidentally.

The next chapter moves from protection to multiplication. It explains how systems expand influence without diluting control.

19

THE MULTIPLIER EFFECT

Wealth that merely survives is fragile. Wealth that multiplies is deliberate. The Multiplier Effect is the point at which systems begin producing more than they consume. It is not growth through exhaustion, but expansion through design. This is how empires spread across ventures, industries, and generations without losing control.

Multiplication is not accidental. It follows rules.

Why Most Expansion Fails

Most people attempt to scale before they stabilize. They add projects, partners, or investments without governance. What looks like growth quickly becomes chaos.

Expansion fails when:

- systems are unclear
- decision authority is vague
- capital is scattered
- identity is not enforced

Multiplication without structure does not compound. It fragments.

The Difference Between Growth and Multiplication

Growth requires effort. Multiplication requires architecture.

Growth looks like working harder, managing more, and being constantly involved. Multiplication looks like delegation, replication, and distance from daily operations.

Empires do not rely on constant supervision. They rely on systems that reproduce outcomes consistently.

The Three Engines of the Multiplier Effect

Every scalable empire relies on three engines working together.

Engine 1: Replicable Systems

A system that works once is not an asset. A system that works repeatedly without degradation is. Replicable systems allow success to be duplicated across locations, people, and time.

Engine 2: Controlled Capital Deployment

Capital is deployed with intention, not emotion. Each new investment is required to strengthen the existing structure, not distract from it. Weak links are removed quickly.

Engine 3: Leadership Multiplication

Empires multiply leaders, not just income. Decision-making authority is trained, tested, and granted selectively. This prevents bottlenecks and preserves standards.

How Wealthy Families Multiply Without Losing Control

Families that endure do not chase every opportunity. They select ventures that align with their existing infrastructure.

Common multiplication strategies include:
- expanding proven business models into new markets
- acquiring complementary businesses rather than unrelated ones
- reinvesting cashflow into adjacent assets
- licensing systems rather than selling control
- using holding companies to centralize ownership

The goal is not volume. It is coherence.

Sample Multiplication Path

(Illustrative Scenario)

To make the Multiplier Effect tangible, it helps to see how some builders apply the principles described in this chapter. What follows is one representative example, not a formula, guarantee, or required plan. The asset types, timing, and sequence are illustrative only.

The purpose of this sample is to demonstrate how credit can be converted into assets, assets into cashflow, and cashflow into equity over time. The logic matters more than the specifics.

Illustrative Move 1 — Income-Producing Real Estate

Some builders choose to begin with one or two rental properties, using business credit strategically for elements such as:

- down payments
- closing costs
- repairs or renovations
- furnishing, where applicable

Over time, appreciation and principal paydown may contribute meaningful equity, often forming an early foundation for portfolio growth.

Illustrative Move 2 — Vehicle-Based or Rental Operations

Others layer in a vehicle-based business, such as a small car rental operation, funded through a combination of business cards and lines of credit. In this model, vehicles function as revenue-generating tools rather than personal purchases, producing monthly cashflow while retaining asset value.

Illustrative Move 3 — Digital or Service-Based Business

Some builders then allocate capital toward a digital or service business, using credit for:

- marketing and advertising
- team support
- systems and infrastructure
- branding or web presence

When structured properly, these businesses can operate independently of the founder's daily labor and may carry significant valuation beyond monthly income.

Illustrative Move 4 — Route-Based or Automated Cashflow Assets

Low-maintenance, route-based businesses such as vending, ATM, or similar operations are sometimes added for stability. These assets are often attractive because of predictable returns and limited operational complexity once established.

Illustrative Move 5 — Brand or E-Commerce Expansion

In some cases, builders expand into brand-based or e-commerce ventures, where valuation is tied to systems, audience, and intellectual property rather than physical inventory alone.

Illustrative Move 6 — Reinvestment and Consolidation

As cashflow increases, profits and available credit are frequently reinvested back into additional real estate or complementary assets. This stage is less about novelty and more about consolidation, strengthening the overall balance sheet and increasing net worth through equity accumulation.

Illustrative Outcome — Portfolio Control

Through repeated application of this logic, some individuals eventually control diversified portfolios with seven-figure net worths — not through savings alone, but through disciplined conversion of:

Credit → Capital → Cashflow → Asset Acquisition → Equity Expansion

This is not the only path. It is simply one way the Multiplier Effect can take shape.

The assets may change. The markets may shift. The principle remains the same.

This sample path exists to clarify possibility, not prescribe behavior. Your path may look entirely different. What matters is that every move serves the same function: converting access into structures that compound. That is how wealth multiplies.

Multiplication Requires Restraint

One of the most counterintuitive truths of empire building is that saying no is often more valuable than saying yes. Every new venture competes for attention, capital, and governance.

Unfuckwithable builders expand only when:

- systems are stable
- leadership is ready
- capital is abundant
- identity is preserved

Anything else is premature.

The Compounding Advantage

When multiplication is executed correctly, momentum accelerates. Each new asset strengthens the next. Cashflow stabilizes risk. Equity expands leverage. Systems reinforce identity.

At this stage, wealth begins behaving like gravity. It attracts opportunity without pursuit.

What This Chapter Advances

This chapter moves the empire from protection to propagation. It shows how disciplined expansion increases influence without eroding control.

The next chapter addresses the final transformation: when a name stops being personal and starts functioning as an institution.

20

THE GOD-TIER VERSION OF YOU — THE FINAL TRANSFORMATION

Becoming wealthy is not the end of the journey. It is the threshold.

The final transformation is not financial. It is personal. Becoming god-tier means you no longer outsource control of your life to circumstance, emotion, or permission. You govern yourself completely. Energy, money, identity, emotion, environment, and future are no longer reactive forces. They are directed.

This is the version of you that controls outcomes instead of negotiating with them. This chapter seals the transformation.

The God-Tier Principles

These principles are not aspirations. They are operating laws. They describe how people move once identity, leverage, and discipline are fully integrated.

Principle 1 — Move Like a Creator, Not a Consumer

Consumers react to what exists. Creators decide what exists next.

God-tier individuals create systems instead of waiting for opportunities. They create wealth instead of chasing income. They create freedom instead of requesting permission. Their life is not something that happens to them. It is something they author.

Principle 2 — Solve Problems, Don't Avoid Them

Problems are not interruptions. They are invitations.

Every problem increases your value, sharpens your skill, and strengthens your identity. Avoidance keeps you small. Engagement makes you formidable. God-tier individuals move toward complexity because complexity is where leverage lives.

Problems are how power is earned.

Principle 3 — Expand Faster Than Life Can Shrink You

Life will apply pressure. Circumstances will test resolve. Doubt will arrive, sometimes from others, sometimes from within.

God-tier individuals do not wait for stability before expanding. They grow faster than resistance can compress them. Expansion becomes their defense.

Principle 4 — Learn Every Day Like Your Life Depends On It

Because it does.

Mistakes turn into wisdom, and failure becomes data when you treat life as a continuous learning cycle, treating each day as an opportunity to gain and apply new knowledge.

One insight can dissolve decades of struggle. One distinction can reroute an entire future. God-tier individuals treat learning as survival, not self-improvement. They compound knowledge daily because stagnation is decay.

Principle 5 — You Are the Architect of Your Reality

Blame is a ceiling.

The moment you stop blaming the system, the government, the people around you, or your past, you reclaim authorship. God-tier control begins where excuses end. Responsibility is not a burden. It is access.

Principle 6 — Wealth Is a Decision First

Before wealth is visible, it is internal.

The moment you decide, *"I will become wealthy,"* your subconscious begins constructing the identity capable of sustaining that decision. Strategy follows commitment. Discipline follows clarity.

Indecision is the true poverty.

Principle 7 — You Will Outgrow Most People

This is not cruelty. It is consequence.

Growth changes frequency. Some relationships cannot survive elevation. God-tier individuals release without resentment. They understand that their future cannot be confined by someone else's limited imagination.

Letting go is part of expansion.

Principle 8 — Silence Is a Weapon

The powerful do not announce intent prematurely.

God-tier individuals move quietly. They build without applause and reveal outcomes only after they are irreversible. Noise is for those seeking validation. Silence is for those accumulating power.

Principle 9 — Your Life Expands to Match Your Self-Worth

Standards dictate outcomes.

Raise your standards and your expectations follow. Raise your expectations and your identity adjusts. Raise your identity and your income has no choice but to respond.

Self-worth is not emotional. It is structural.

Principle 10 — The Universe Rewards the Bold

Momentum favors movement.

When you take bold action, conditions rearrange. Doors open. People appear. Opportunities multiply. What looks like magic is often simply the consequence of decisive motion sustained over time.

God-tier individuals do not wait for certainty. They create it.

21

WHEN YOUR NAME WILL CARRY WEIGHT

There comes a point when wealth stops being something you manage and becomes something that moves ahead of you. This is the moment when your name carries weight.

A weighted name opens doors before you arrive. It earns trust without explanation. It signals credibility, stability, and expectation. At this level, money is no longer the loudest thing in the room. Reputation is.

This is the final evolution.

The Difference Between Recognition and Weight

Recognition is visibility. Weight is authority.

Many people are known. Few are trusted. Recognition can be built quickly through noise, marketing, or momentary success. Weight is earned slowly through consistency, restraint, and follow-through.

A name with weight does not need to announce itself. It is referenced quietly, respected instinctively, and defended when absent.

How a Name Gains Weight

Names gain weight through behavior, not branding. Weight is built when:

- commitments are honored without exception
- systems operate reliably over time
- decisions remain steady under pressure
- partnerships improve outcomes rather than complicate them
- values are enforced even when inconvenient

People trust what behaves predictably. Institutions invest in what endures.

The Institutional Shift

At this stage, you are no longer perceived as an individual operator. You are seen as an institution. Banks respond differently. Partners listen more carefully. Opportunities arrive pre-structured.

This is not favoritism. It is risk assessment.

A name with weight lowers uncertainty. Lower uncertainty attracts capital.

Why Loud Wealth Fades and Quiet Wealth Endures

Flash attracts attention. Stability attracts longevity.

Those who perform wealth often feel compelled to prove it repeatedly. Those whose names carry weight have nothing to prove. Their presence alone signals capacity.

Quiet wealth compounds because it is not busy defending itself.

Responsibility That Comes With Weight

When your name carries weight, your decisions affect more than your own outcome. They influence employees, families, communities, and future generations.

This responsibility requires restraint. It demands foresight. It requires saying no to opportunities that compromise integrity, even when they are profitable.

Weight is lost faster than it is gained.

Teaching the Next Generation

A name that carries weight must be taught, not assumed. The next generation must understand what the name represents, what it protects, and what it requires.

This is how institutions survive founders. The name becomes a standard, not a personality.

The Final Truth

Wealth is temporary without structure. Power is temporary without discipline. Influence is temporary without character. However, a name that carries weight can outlast markets, trends, and lifetimes. That is the true measure of success.

Closing the Circle

This book began with access. It ends with authority.

You now understand how credit works, how leverage is built, how systems scale, how identity stabilizes power, and how legacy is designed to endure. What you do with this knowledge determines what follows.

Your name is already being written into the future. The only question is whether it will be remembered as noise… or as weight.

www.ingramcontent.com/pod-product-compliance
Lightning Source LLC
Chambersburg PA
CBHW061738050726
47598CB00002B/527